Reduce, Reuse, Recycle

Water

Alexandra Fix

Heinemann
LIBRARY

www.heinemann.co.uk/library
Visit our website to find out more information about **Heinemann Library** books.

To order:

 Phone ++44 (0)1865 888066

 Send a fax to ++44 (0)1865 314091

 Visit the Heinemann Bookshop at www.heinemann.co.uk/library to browse our catalogue and order online.

First published in Great Britain by Heinemann Library, Halley Court, Jordan Hill, Oxford OX2 8EJ, part of Harcourt Education.
Heinemann is a registered trademark of Harcourt Education Ltd.

Editorial: Cassie Mayer and Diyan Leake
Design: Steven Mead and Debbie Oatley
Picture research: Ruth Blair
Production: Duncan Gilbert

Origination: Chroma Graphics (Overseas) Pte Ltd
Printed and bound in China by South China Printing Company Ltd

ISBN 978 0 431 90759 8
12 11 10 09 08

10 9 8 7 6 5 4 3 2 1

British Library Cataloguing in Publication Data
Fix, Alexandra, 1950-
   Water. - (Reduce, reuse, recycle)
   1. Sewage - Juvenile literature 2. Water reuse - Juvenile literature 3. Waste minimization - Juvenile literature
   I. Title
   363.7'284

Acknowledgements
The publishers would like to thank the following for permission to reproduce photographs: Alamy pp. **24** (Keith M. Law), **27** (Paul Glendell), **28** (Rob Wilkinson); Corbis pp. **4**, **7**, **18** (Carl & Ann Purcell), **21**, **22**, **23** (Jean Louis Atlan/Sygma), **26** (George Shelley/Michael Keller); Getty Images pp. **10** (Michael Salas), **11** (Flip Chalfant), **12** (Stone/Paul Chesley), **13**, **15** (Iconica/Ashley Karyl), **16** (Photographer's Choice/Aura), **17** (Taxi/Gen Nishino), **20** (Stone/John Edwards), **25** (Photographer's Choice/Oliver Strewe); Ginny Stroud-Lewis p. **19**; Science Photo Library pp. **6** (Gusto Images), **9** (Christian Darkin), **14** (Chris Knapton).

Cover photograph reproduced with permission of Alamy (Tim Graham).

The publishers would like to thank Simon Miller for his assistance in the preparation of this book.

Every effort has been made to contact copyright holders of any material reproduced in this book. Any omissions will be rectified in subsequent printings if notice is given to the publishers.

Contents

Some words are shown in bold, **like this**. You can find out what they mean by looking in the glossary.

Why is water important?

Three-quarters of the earth is covered by water. Most of this water is salt water from the oceans. Only a very small part is fresh water that we can use in our homes.

The earth looks blue from space because of water in the oceans and in the air.

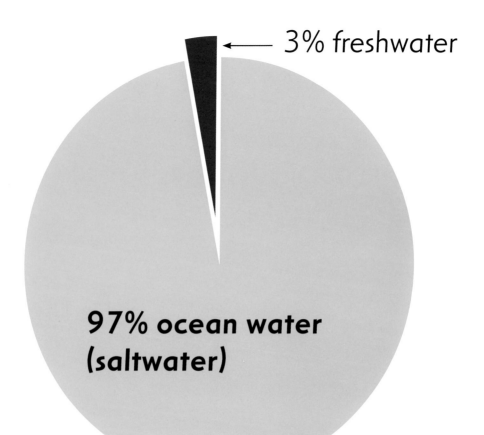

3% freshwater

97% ocean water
(saltwater)

Much of the earth's fresh water is
locked in ice caps and glaciers.

We use water to drink, take showers, clean
dishes, and grow food. We need to use
water every day, but there are many ways
to use less water.

How do we use water?

More than half of your body is made up of water. You need to drink lots of water every day.

A person could only live for a few days without water.

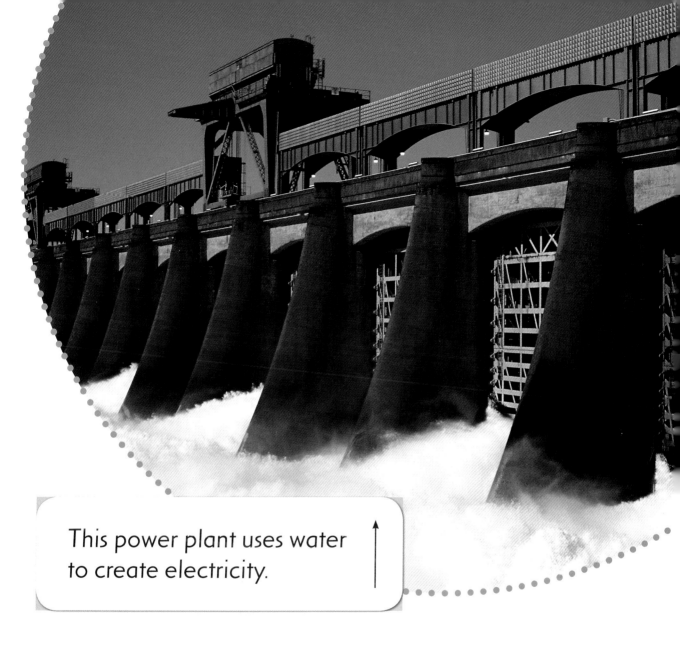

This power plant uses water to create electricity.

Farmers use water to grow plants. Firefighters need water to put out fires. We can also use water to make **electricity**.

Where does water come from?

Water is always in motion around the earth. It changes form, but does not disappear. This constant motion and change is called the **water cycle**.

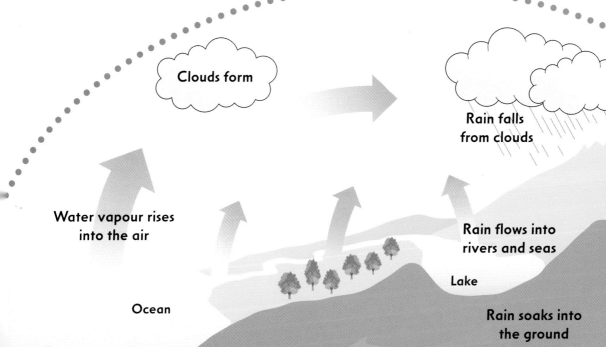

Clouds form

Rain falls from clouds

Water vapour rises into the air

Rain flows into rivers and seas

Lake

Ocean

Rain soaks into the ground

Rain that fell on dinosaurs millions of years ago is the same rain that falls today.

The heat from the sun shines on lakes, oceans, and rivers. This heat changes water into a gas called **water vapour**. The gas rises into the air and forms clouds. Clouds return water to earth as rain, snow, or sleet.

How does water get to our homes?

The water that we use comes from lakes, rivers, and underground **aquifers**. Before we use water from these sources, it must be taken to a **water treatment plant**.

This is the inside of a water treatment plant.

This man is cleaning the water at a treatment plant. ↑

At a water treatment plant, water is made clean enough to drink. The clean water is carried by underground pipes to our homes for use in sinks, baths, and showers.

Will we always have water?

Water falls from clouds as rain, sleet, or snow. ↑

Water is a **renewable resource**. It moves from the land to the clouds and back to the land again. It changes form but does not disappear.

Some parts of the world have enough water, but their water sources can become **polluted**. The water is too dirty to drink safely. Some parts of the world have very little water. They do not have enough water to drink or to grow crops.

People need clean drinking water to stay alive and healthy.

What happens when we waste water?

Water that is dumped down a sink or toilet must be cleaned at a **waste water treatment plant**. This uses a form of **energy** called **electricity**.

After dirty water is cleaned, it is returned to the sea, lakes, and rivers.

If clean water is poured down the drain, it mixes with dirty water.

If we waste less water, not as much water will have to be cleaned. This will save energy.

How can we reduce water waste?

We can reduce water waste by using less water. When you get water from a tap, pour only what you will drink. Never leave a tap running.

Do not run water to get it cold. Instead, keep a jug of water in the fridge.

Turn off the tap when you brush your teeth.

Use clothing and towels more than once. Washing machines use water to clean clothes and towels. If we wash items less often we will reduce water waste.

How can we reuse water?

There are many ways to reuse water. If you are not going to finish a glass of water, do not pour it down the sink. Instead, water a plant with your leftover water.

Collect rainwater in a bucket to water flowers on a hot, dry day.

Use old washing-up water to rinse items for **recycling**.

You can water bushes or outdoor plants with old washing-up water. The soap left in the water will help the ground soak up the water.

What is recycled water?

These tanks remove solids from dirty water. ↑

After water is cleaned at a **waste water treatment plant**, it is often sent back to rivers. Water can be reused before it returns to that body of water. This is sometimes called **recycled** water.

Recycled water can be used to water farmland. The water soaks into the ground and then flows back to lakes, rivers, or streams.

Watering crops is a good way to use recycled water.

What is water pollution?

Water **pollution** is when poisons get into the water supply. This can happen when waste or chemicals are dumped into rivers or lakes. The water becomes unsafe to drink.

Polluted water can kill animals and fish.

When ships carrying oil crash, people must act fast to control the damage to plants and animals.

We must keep our water sources clean so we will always have the water we need. Polluted water can make people sick. It must be cleaned before it can be used.

How can we reduce water pollution?

To keep water clean, we must not add harmful things to it. Anything dumped on the ground, in the water, or down a sink or toilet can harm water.

Water from storm drains goes right into streams or rivers.

Compost can be added to soil to help plants grow.

Do not put leftover food scraps down the sink. The food waste **pollutes** water. Instead, create a **compost** heap. A compost heap is a collection of food waste that eventually rots away.

How can you take action?

You can help reduce water waste. Remind family and friends of ways to use water wisely. Make sure you use only the water you need.

Use a watering can instead of a hose to save water.

It is important to pick up litter from bodies of water.

You can help keep our water clean. Be careful not to put harmful things into water. Never throw rubbish into lakes or rivers.

Does a shower waste less water than a bath?

The next time you take a shower, close the plug and let the water collect in the bath. When your shower is finished, see how much water is in the bath. Does a shower or a bath use more water?

Does a bath use more or less water than a shower?

Fast facts

You waste around 7.5 litres of water each time you leave the water running while you brush your teeth.

Salt water from the sea can be turned into fresh drinking water by removing the salt. This is called desalination.

About 500 million people live in areas of the world where there is not enough water.

Taking a bath uses around twice as much water as taking a short shower.

Glossary

aquifer   layer of rock, sand, or gravel that holds water under ground

compost   food scraps and plant waste that can be added to soil

electricity   form of energy used to create light, heat, and power

energy   power to do work

pollute   fill with harmful or poisonous substances

pollution   wastes and poisons in the air, water, or soil

recycle   process and reuse

renewable resource   material of the earth that can be replaced

waste water treatment plant   place where water from sinks and toilets goes to be cleaned before it is returned to rivers and streams

water cycle   constant movement of water between sky, land, and sea

water treatment plant   place where water is taken from lakes, rivers, and streams to be cleaned for use in homes

water vapour   tiny drops of water that float in the air and form clouds

Find out more

Books to read

The Life and Times of a Drop of Water: The Water Cycle, Angela Royston (Raintree, 2006)

One World, Michael Foreman (Andersen Press, 2004)

Using Materials: How We Use Water, Chris Oxlade (Raintree, 2005)

Websites

Waste Watch work to teach people about reducing, reusing, and recycling waste. You can visit www.recyclezone.org.uk to find out more information about waste and to try some online activities..

Find out where you can recycle in your local area at: www.recyclenow.com by typing in your postcode. You can also find out more about which items can be recycled, more facts about waste, and what you can do to help!

Index